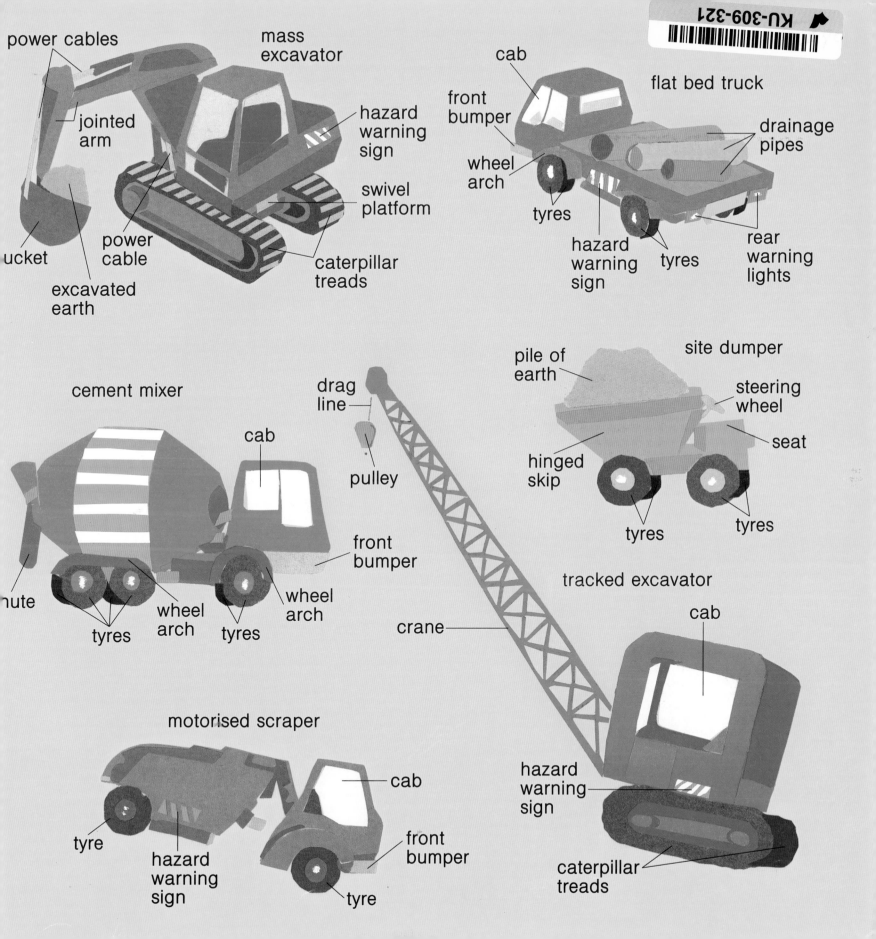

For Lisa, with love   ST

For Peter   AA

Text copyright © 1997 Sue Tarsky
Illustrations copyright © 1997 Alex Ayliffe

First published in 1997 by **ABC**, All Books for Children,
a division of The All Children's Company Ltd,
33 Museum Street, London WC1A 1LD

Printed and bound in Hong Kong

British Library Cataloguing in Publication Data
Tarsky, Sue
The busy building book
1.Buildings - Juvenile literature 2.Skyscrapers - Design
and construction - Juvenile literature
I.Title II.Ayliffe, Alex
721

ISBN 1-85406-241-7

The Busy Building Book

words by **Sue Tarsky**

pictures by **Alex Ayliffe**

ABC
London

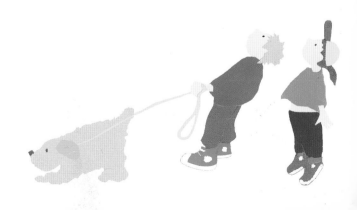

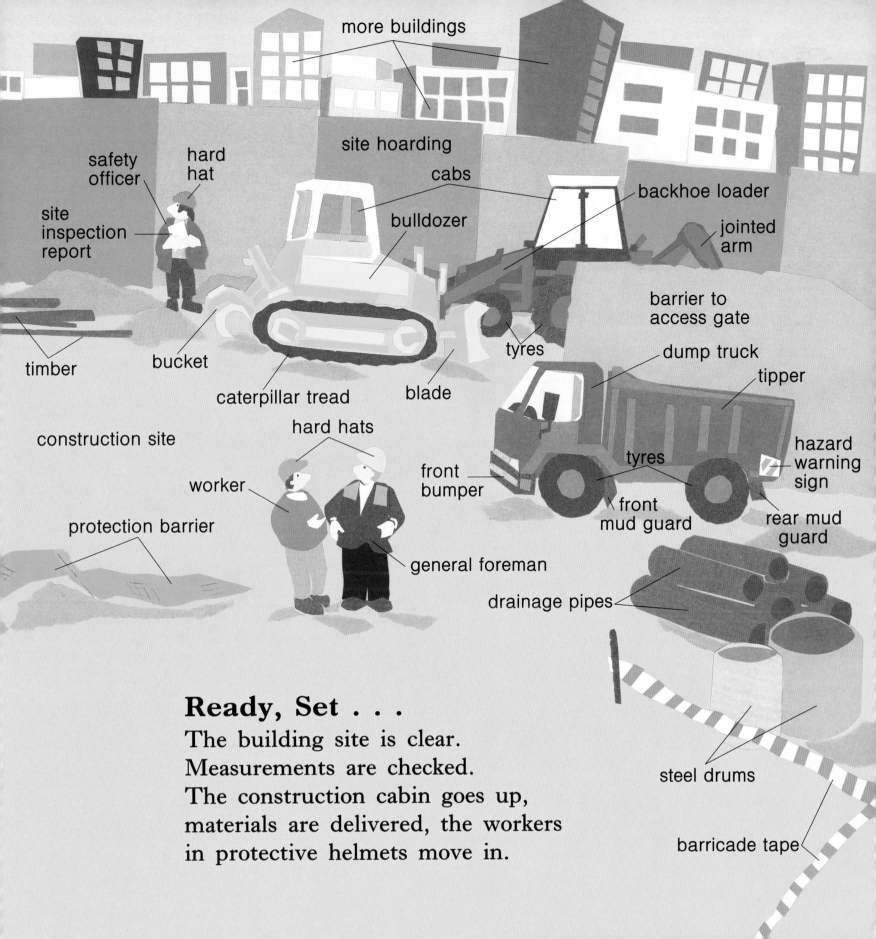

more buildings

site hoarding

cabs

backhoe loader

jointed arm

safety officer

hard hat

site inspection report

bulldozer

barrier to access gate

dump truck

tipper

timber

bucket

caterpillar tread

blade

tyres

construction site

hard hats

worker

front bumper

tyres

hazard warning sign

protection barrier

general foreman

front mud guard

rear mud guard

drainage pipes

Ready, Set . . .

The building site is clear.
Measurements are checked.
The construction cabin goes up,
materials are delivered, the workers
in protective helmets move in.

steel drums

barricade tape

Excavate!

Before the building goes up, it has to go down. Workers dig a big hole for the foundations, the part of the building that's underground, and helps hold it up.

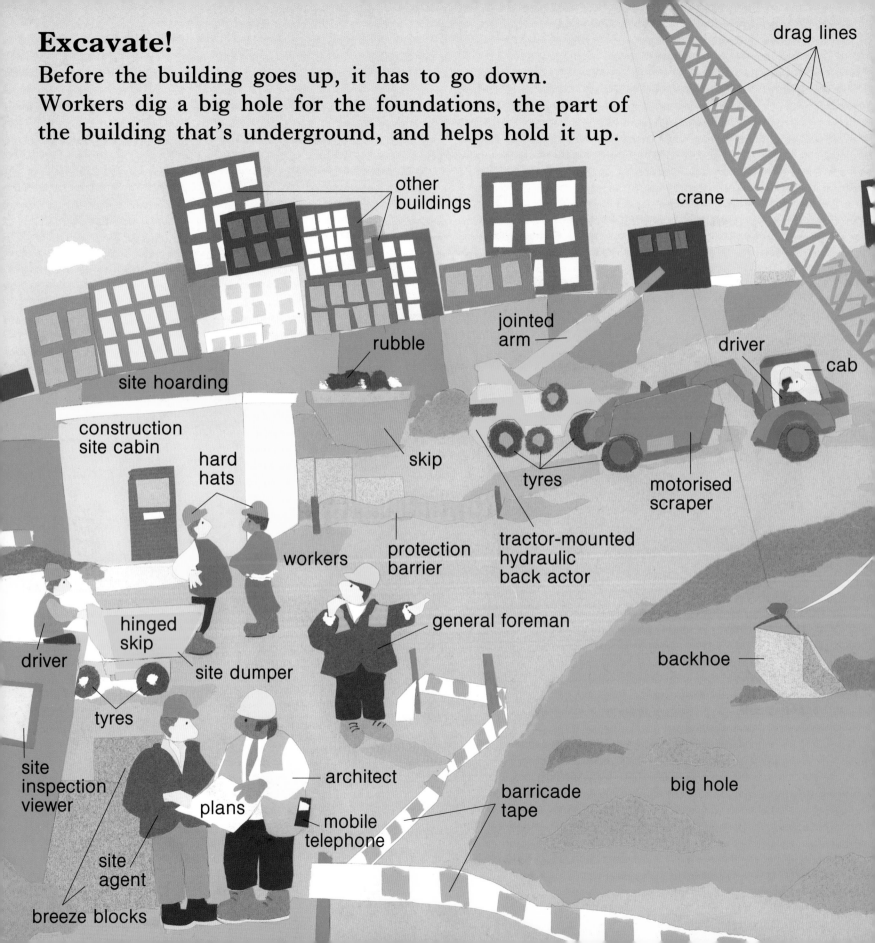

drag lines

other buildings

crane

jointed arm

driver

cab

rubble

site hoarding

construction site cabin

hard hats

skip

tyres

motorised scraper

workers

protection barrier

tractor-mounted hydraulic back actor

hinged skip

general foreman

backhoe

driver

site dumper

tyres

architect

barricade tape

big hole

site inspection viewer

plans

mobile telephone

site agent

breeze blocks

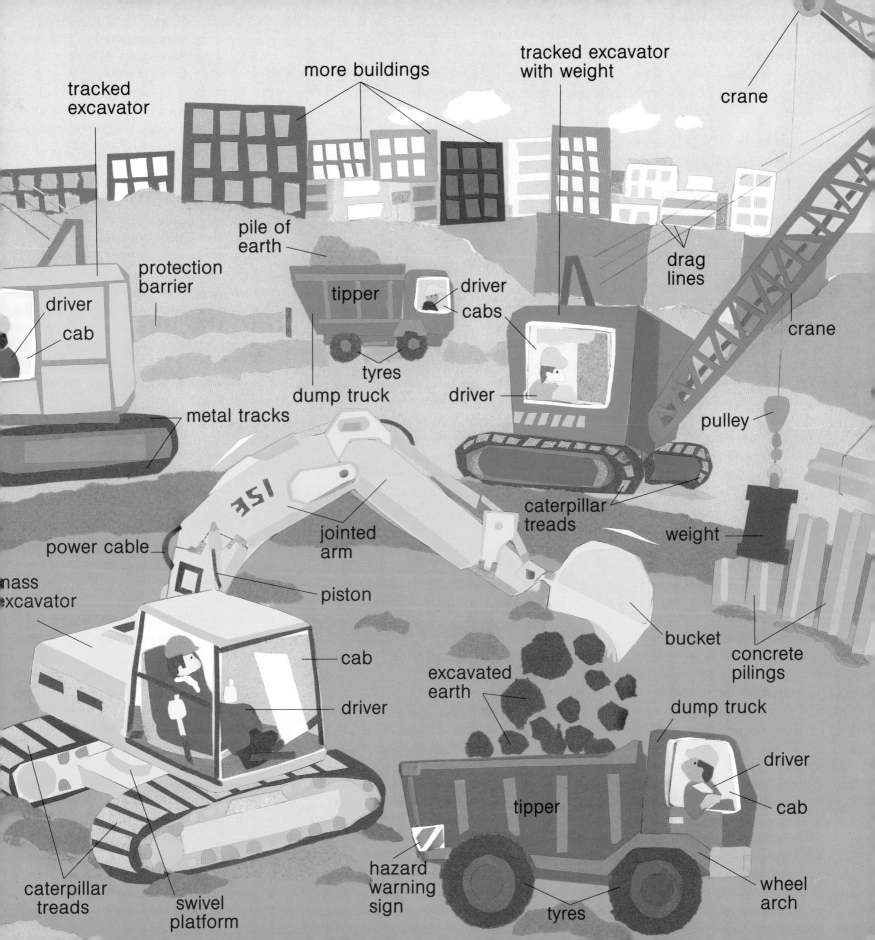

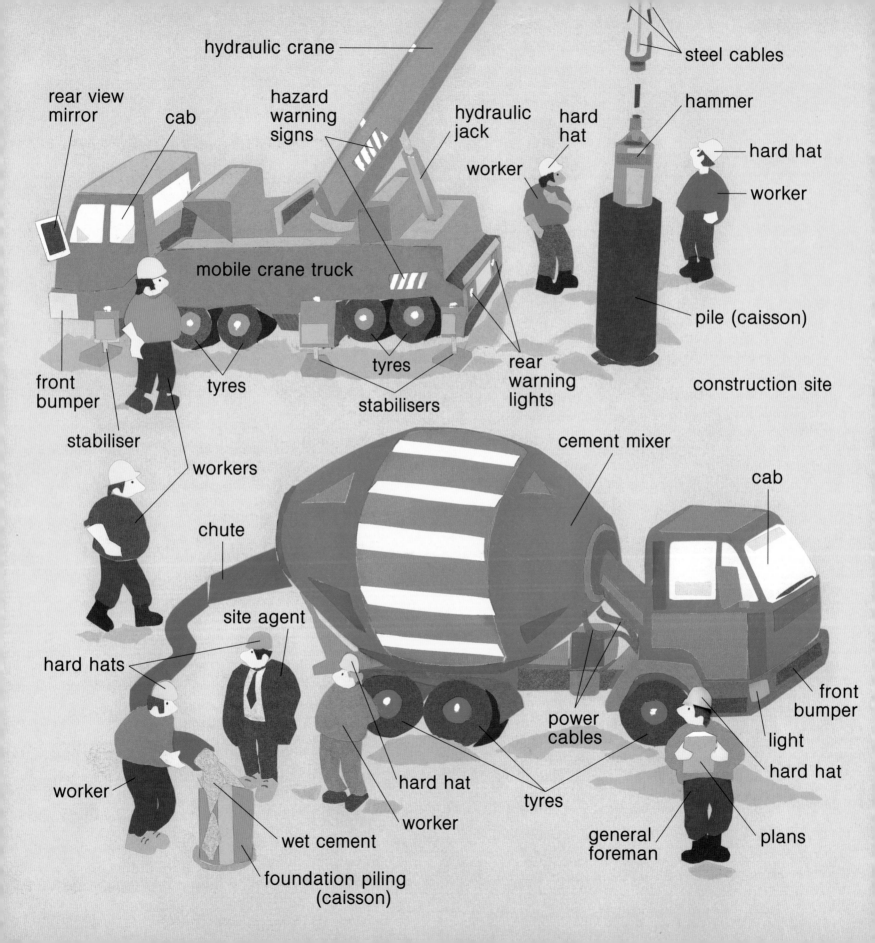

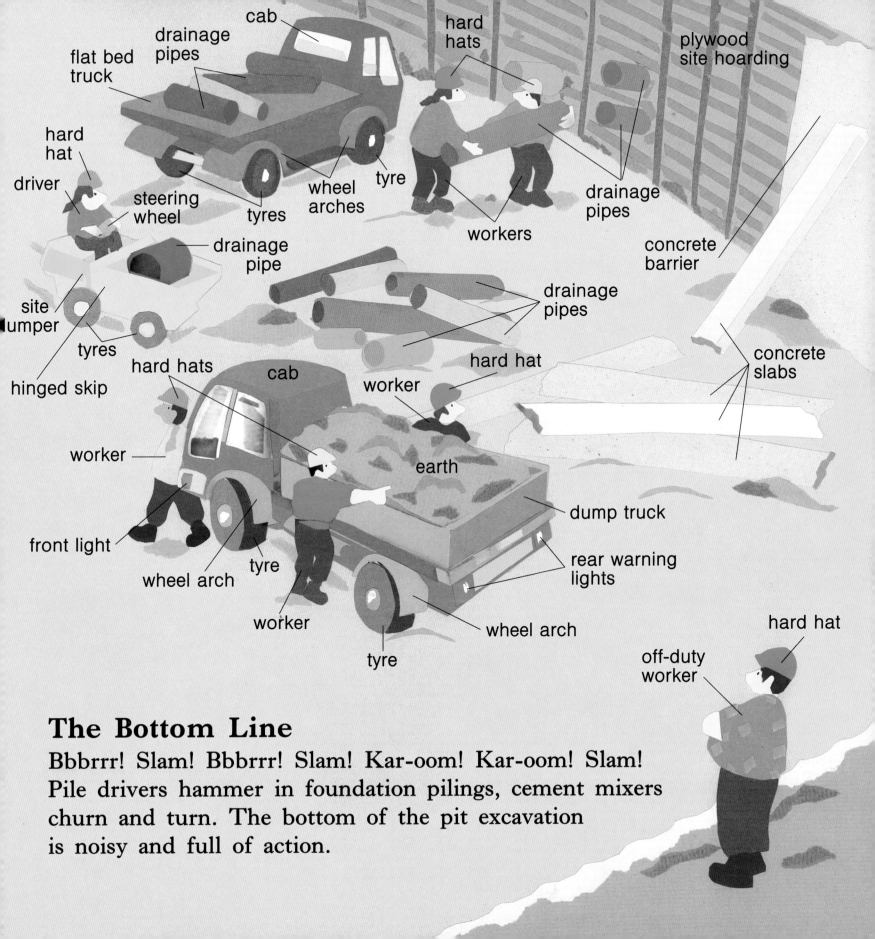

cab

drainage pipes

flat bed truck

hard hats

plywood site hoarding

hard hat

driver

steering wheel

tyres

wheel arches

tyre

workers

drainage pipes

concrete barrier

drainage pipe

drainage pipes

site dumper

tyres

hard hat

hinged skip

concrete slabs

hard hats

cab

worker

worker

earth

dump truck

front light

wheel arch

tyre

rear warning lights

worker

wheel arch

tyre

off-duty worker

hard hat

The Bottom Line

Bbbrrr! Slam! Bbbrrr! Slam! Kar-oom! Kar-oom! Slam!
Pile drivers hammer in foundation pilings, cement mixers
churn and turn. The bottom of the pit excavation
is noisy and full of action.

Going Up!

Scaffolding starts to rise, and so does the skeleton of the building. People and machines are busy everywhere, taking away earth, delivering materials.

tower scaffold

other buildings

pile of earth

backhoe loader

hard hat

site hoarding

driver

tipper

breeze blocks

tyre

scaffold couplers

cab

site inspection viewer

site inspection viewer

site hoarding

shopper

site hoarding

friends

bicycle

bag

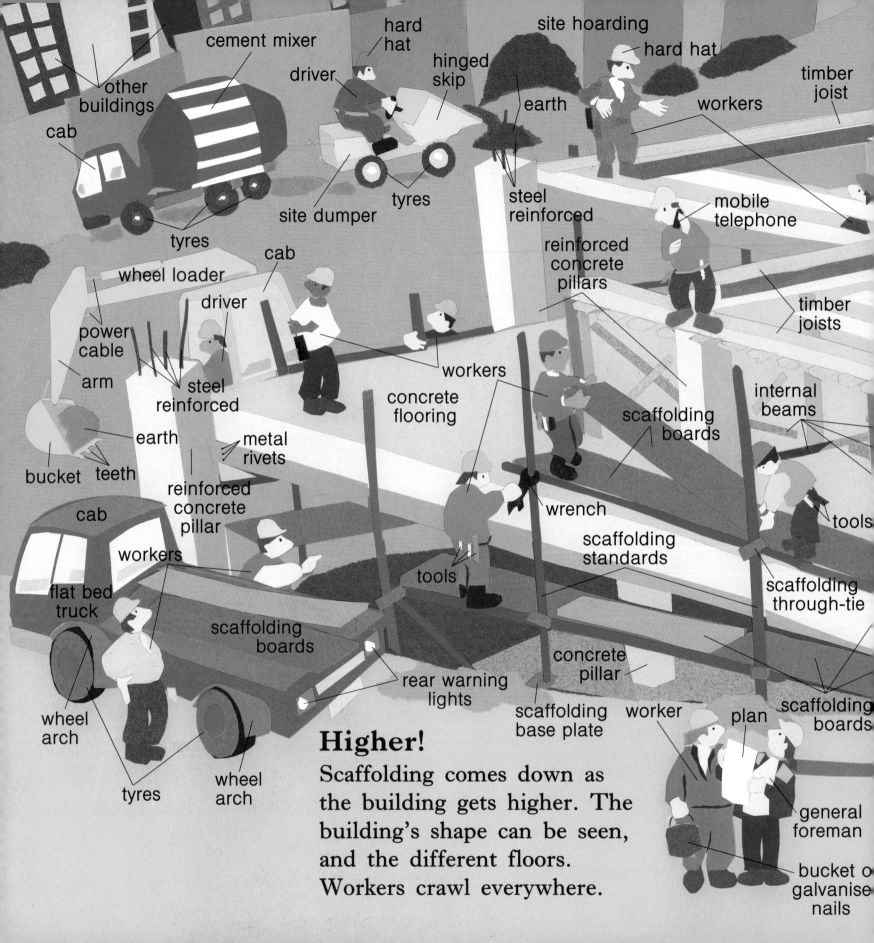

Higher!

Scaffolding comes down as the building gets higher. The building's shape can be seen, and the different floors. Workers crawl everywhere.

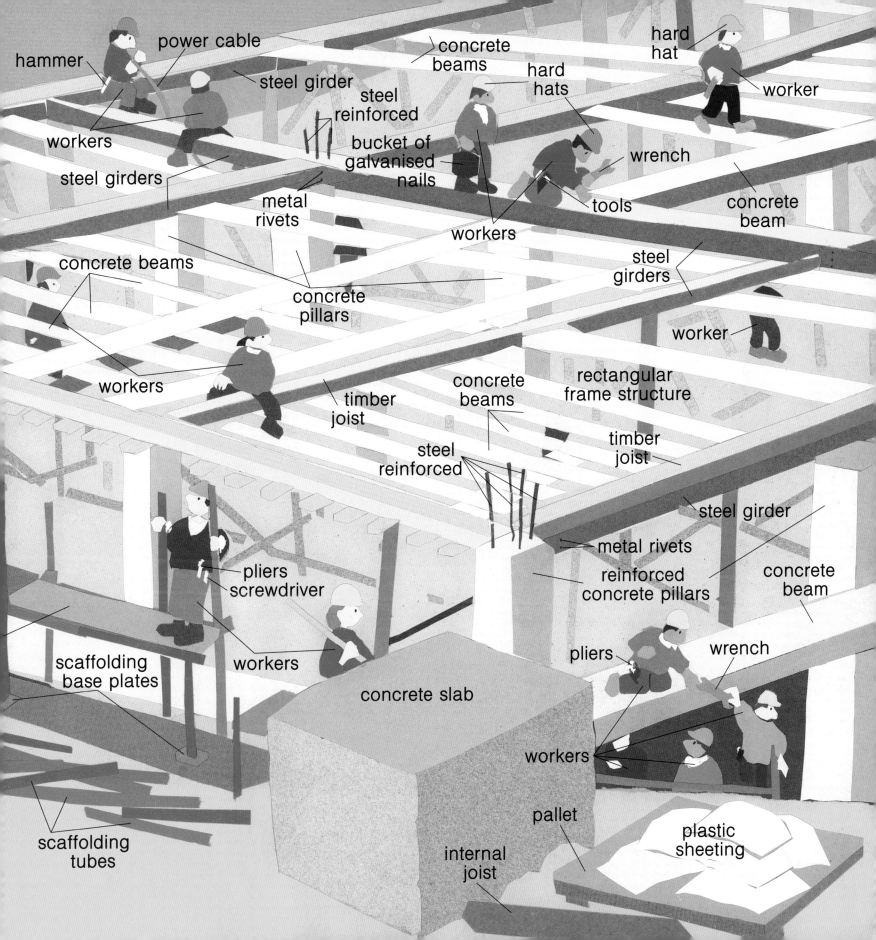

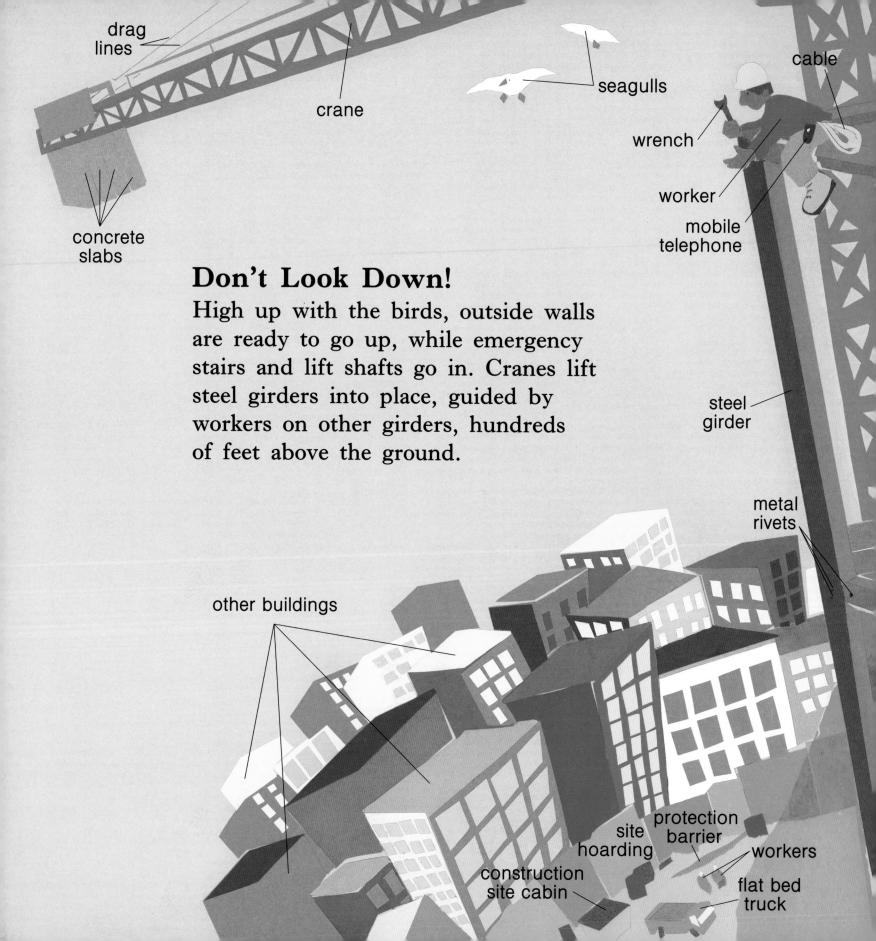

drag lines

crane

seagulls

cable

wrench

worker

mobile telephone

concrete slabs

Don't Look Down!

High up with the birds, outside walls are ready to go up, while emergency stairs and lift shafts go in. Cranes lift steel girders into place, guided by workers on other girders, hundreds of feet above the ground.

steel girder

metal rivets

other buildings

protection barrier

site hoarding

workers

construction site cabin

flat bed truck

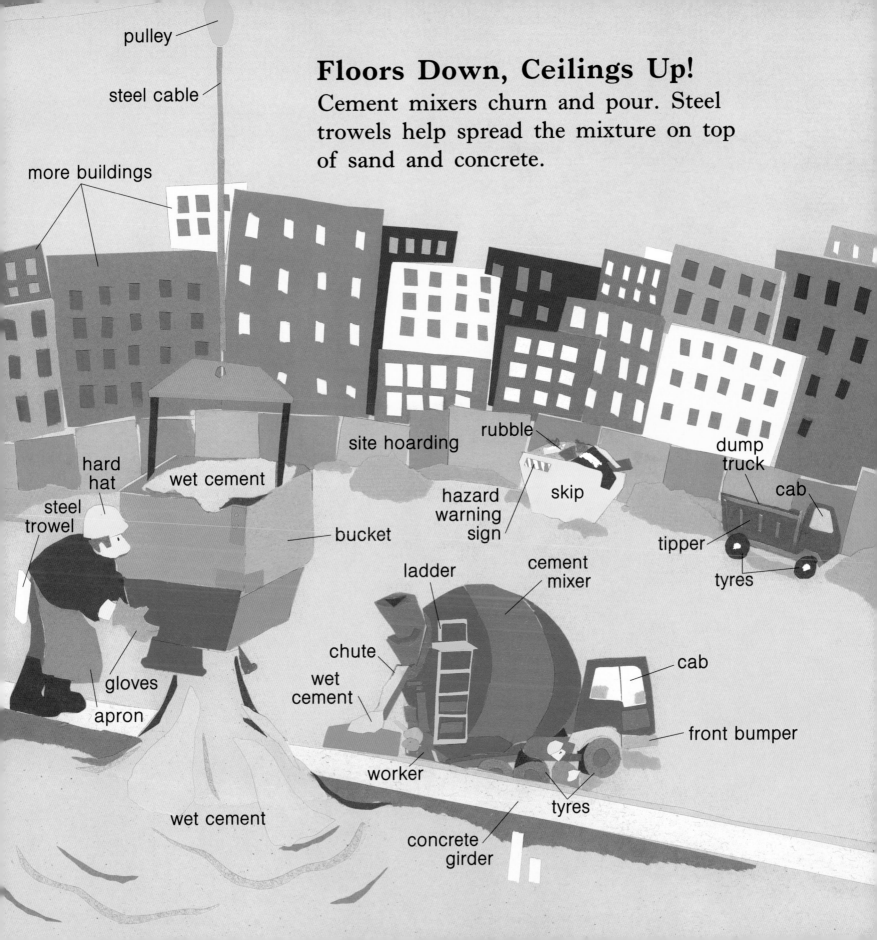

Floors Down, Ceilings Up!

Cement mixers churn and pour. Steel trowels help spread the mixture on top of sand and concrete.

pulley

steel cable

more buildings

site hoarding

rubble

dump truck

hard hat

wet cement

hazard warning sign

skip

cab

steel trowel

bucket

tipper

gloves

ladder

cement mixer

tyres

apron

chute

wet cement

cab

worker

front bumper

wet cement

tyres

concrete girder

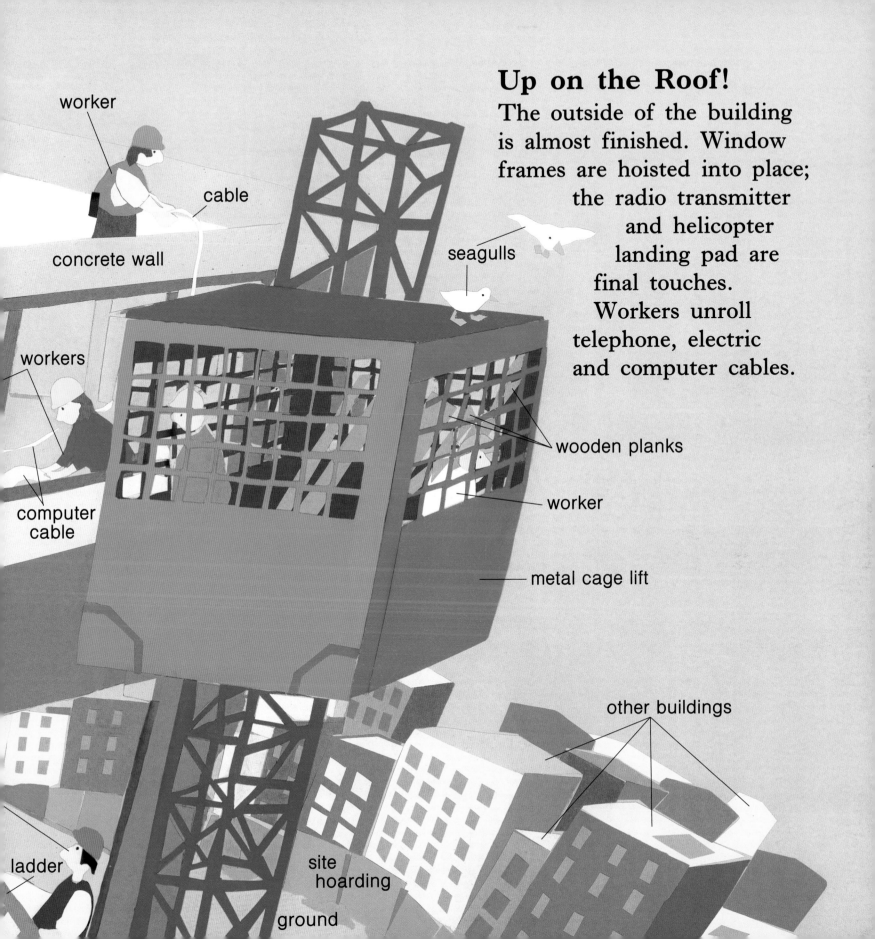

worker

cable

concrete wall

seagulls

Up on the Roof!
The outside of the building is almost finished. Window frames are hoisted into place; the radio transmitter and helicopter landing pad are final touches. Workers unroll telephone, electric and computer cables.

workers

wooden planks

worker

computer cable

metal cage lift

other buildings

ladder

site hoarding

ground

workers

doorway

worker

screwdriver

pencil

hard hat

hard hat

sheet of plaster board

paper

worker

mug of coffee

sacks of insulation

tape

hammer

sack of insulation

wrench

wooden planks

tool chest

clipboard

empty storage bin

screwdriver

workers

worker's bag

computer cable

sheet of plaster board

table top

worker

workers

wooden plank

wrench

workers

wrench

architect

blue prints

Saw, Hammer, Drill!
The electricity is on. Wooden struts go up and, when sheets of plaster board are nailed to them, there are walls and rooms.

table top

hammer

wooden plank

insulation worker

cable

concrete walls

insulation

steel cable

electric cables

plaster board wall

roll of insulation

electric cable drum

electric cable

closed tool box

electric cable

concrete floor

cable junction boxes

floor cavity

cable junction boxes

plumbing pipe

painted plaster board walls

hammer

insulation

Room at the Top!

Hot air, cold air, running water; doors, carpets, ceilings, walls; toilets, sinks, taps - lifts carry it all.

wooden planks

lift

wooden door frame

plaster board walls

worker

step ladder

sink

toilet seat lid

piece of wood

part of wooden door

other part of door

toilet

computer cable drum

awl

closed tool box

wooden planks

painted floor

file

floor cavity

floor cavity

cable junction boxes

plaster board walls

piece of painted wood

plaster board walls

lift shaft

concrete wall

wooden planks

insulation

insulation

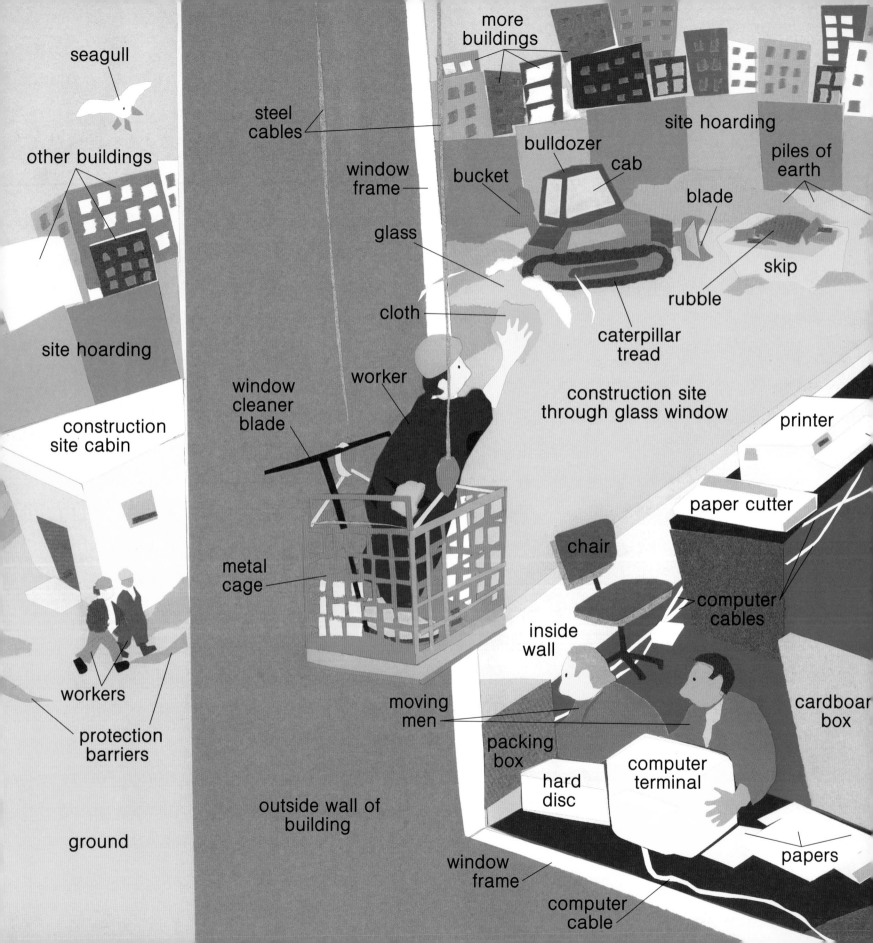

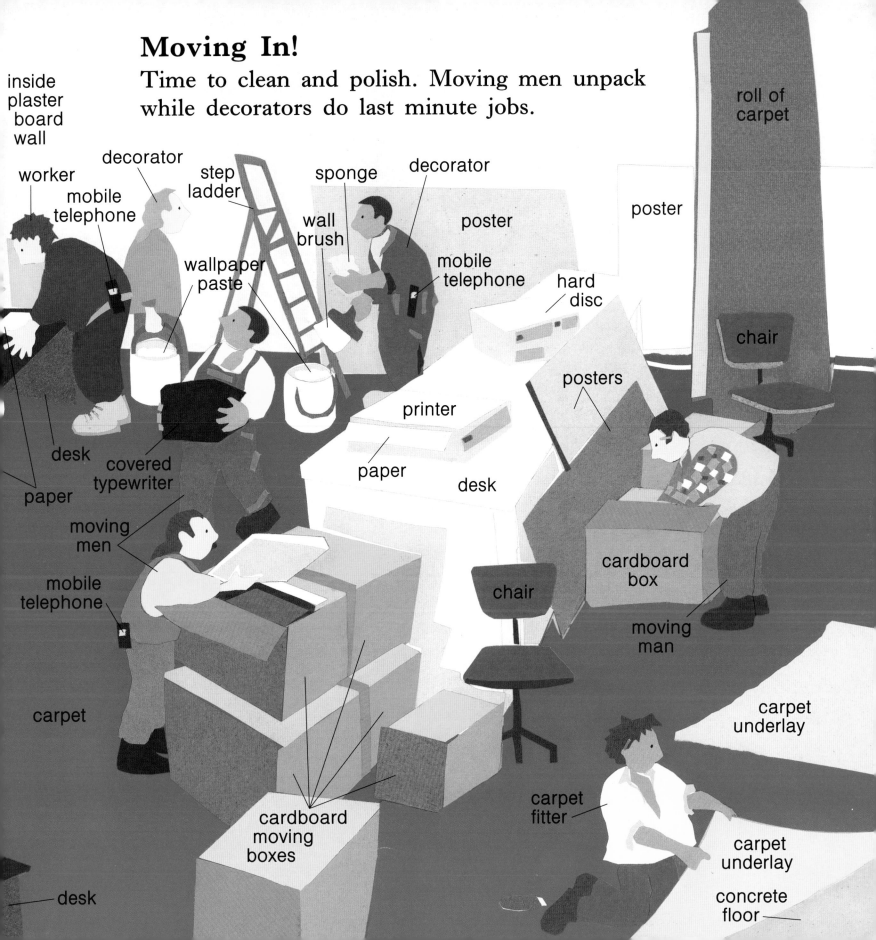

Moving In!

Time to clean and polish. Moving men unpack while decorators do last minute jobs.

inside plaster board wall

worker

decorator

step ladder

sponge

decorator

roll of carpet

poster

mobile telephone

wall brush

poster

wallpaper paste

mobile telephone

poster

hard disc

chair

printer

posters

desk

covered typewriter

paper

desk

paper

moving men

mobile telephone

carpet

chair

cardboard box

moving man

carpet underlay

carpet fitter

cardboard moving boxes

carpet underlay

desk

concrete floor

Done!

It has taken a long time, but the building is finished. The owners give speeches while office staff listen, ready to start work in their new building.

all the other buildings

trees

tree

cars

crowd of people

traffic jams

road

concrete wall

finished building

windows

outside structure

windows

The Busy Building

outside structure

side doors

front doors

another crowd of people

the owners

front steps

landscaped site

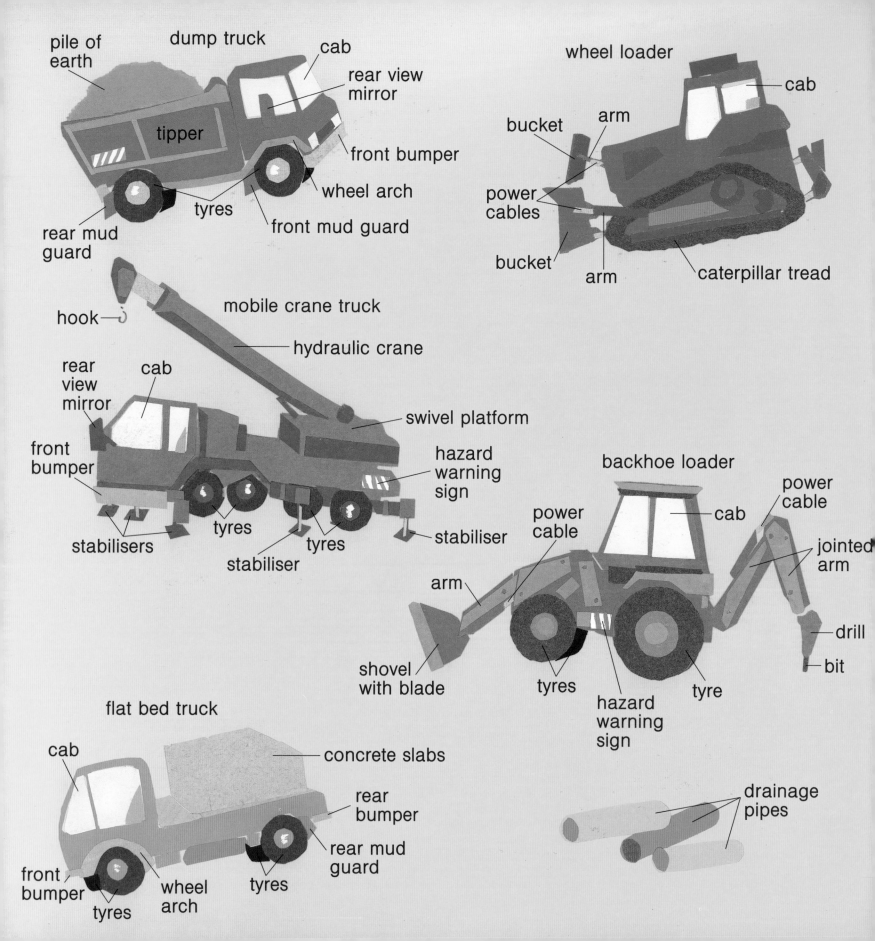